ing of the
-Australia Flight
MY JOHNSON.
AMY
Jason
WORDS BY
JOS GEO
GILBERT
MUSIC BY
HORATIO
NICHOLLS
Lawrence Wright
PRICE 6D NET
PRINTED IN ENGLAND

AMY JOHN (Song Sheet), 1930
© Martin Breese/Retrograph Archive 1995
Copyright © Studio Designs 1995

VICKERS 618 WELLINGTON T.10
RAF MUSEUM, HENDON, UK
© Austin Brown/The Aviation Picture Library 1995
Copyright © Studio Designs 1995

B·O·A·C ROLLS-ROYCE **707**

LONDON * NEW YORK * MONTREAL * TORONTO

BOAC 707, 1959
© Martin Breese/Retrograph Archive 1995
Copyright © Studio Designs 1995

JAVELIN AIRCRAFT
© e.t.archive, London 1995
Copyright © Studio Designs 1995

BRITISH AEROSPACE HARRIER GR5
1SQDN RAF WITTERING, FARNBOROUGH, UK
© Austin Brown/The Aviation Picture Library 1995
Copyright © Studio Designs 1995

B2 STEALTH BOMBER
NORTHROP, PALMDALE, USA
© Austin Brown/The Aviation Picture Library 1995
Copyright © Studio Designs 1995

HISTOIRE DES BALLONS.

CENTRAL AIRLINES: STINSON "A"

UNITED AIRLINES: DOUGLAS D.C.3

IMPERIAL AIRWAYS LINER "SCYLLA"

DEUTSCHE LUFT HANSA: HEINKEL HE.70

SWISSAIR: DOUGLAS D.C.2

PAN AMERICAN AIRWAYS: GLENN MARTIN 130 FLYING-BOAT "CHINA CLIPPER"

UNITED AIRLINES: DOUGLAS D.C.3
CENTRAL AIRLINES: STINSON 'A'
PAN AM: GLENN MARTIN 130 FLYING-BOAT 'CHINA CLIPPER'
IMPERIAL AIRWAYS LINER 'SCYLLA'
SWISSAIR: DOUGLAS D.C.2
DEUTSCHE LUFT HANSA: HEINKEL HE.70

5¢

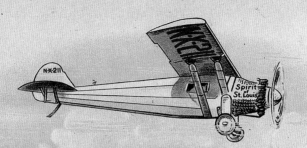

FIRST FLIGHT–NEW YORK TO PARIS–MAY 20–21,1927–33½ HOURS

Spirit of St.Louis

NEW YORK

ST.LOUIS

PARIS

LONG FILLER IMPORTED SUMATRA WRAPPER

REG. U.S. PAT. OFF.

AMERICAN LITHOGRAPHIC CO.,N.Y. U.S.A.

SPIRIT OF ST LOUIS (Cigar Label), American 1927
© Martin Breese/Retrograph Archive 1995
Copyright © Studio Designs 1995

LINDBERGH
(THE EAGLE OF THE U.S.A)

by HOWARD JOHNSON & AL SHERMAN

Shapiro, Bernstein & Co.
MUSIC PUBLISHERS
Cor. Broadway & 47th Street
New York.

MADE IN U.S.A.

AMY

GRAHAM

WORDS BY
JOS GEO GILBERT

MUSIC BY
HORATIO NICHOLLS

6D

MY JOHNSON

PRINTED IN ENGLAND

VICKERS 618 WELLINGTON T.10
RAF MUSEUM, HENDON, UK
© Austin Brown/The Aviation Picture Library 1995
Copyright © Studio Designs 1995

B·O·A·C ROLLS-ROYCE 707

LONDON * NEW YORK * MONTREAL * TORONTO

BOAC 707, 1959
© Martin Breese/Retrograph Archive 1995
Copyright © Studio Designs 1995

CENTRAL AIRLINES: STINSON "A"

UNITED AIRLINES: DOUGLAS D.C. 3

IMPERIAL AIRWAYS LINER "SCYLLA"

DEUTSCHE LUFT HANSA: HEINKEL HE. 70

SWISSAIR: DOUGLAS D.C. 2

PAN AMERICAN AIRWAYS: GLENN MARTIN 130 FLYING-BOAT "CHINA CLIPPER"

UNITED AIRLINES: DOUGLAS D.C.3
CENTRAL AIRLINES: STINSON 'A'
PAN AM: GLENN MARTIN 130 FLYING-BOAT 'CHINA CLIPPER'
IMPERIAL AIRWAYS LINER 'SCYLLA'
SWISSAIR: DOUGLAS D.C.2
DEUTSCHE LUFT HANSA: HEINKEL HE.70

5¢

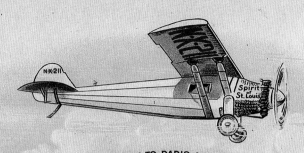

FIRST FLIGHT-NEW YORK TO PARIS-MAY 20-21,1927-33½ HOURS

Spirit
of St. Louis

NEW YORK

PARIS

ST. LOUIS

LONG FILLER IMPORTED SUMATRA WRAPPER

LINDBERGH
(THE EAGLE OF THE U.S.A.)

by HOWARD JOHNSON & AL SHERMAN

Made by Shapiro, Bernstein & Co.
MUSIC PUBLISHERS
Broadway & 47th Street
New York

MADE IN U.S.A.